WHY CAN'T EVERY DAY BE DADDY DAY?

- A Christian Story of Separation and Divorce

By: JoAnn LaForte & Joshua A. Young

Illustrator: Arif Khan of India

This is a work of fiction. The events and characters described herein are imaginary and are not intended to refer to specific places or living persons. The opinions expressed in this manuscript are solely the opinions of the authors and do not represent the opinions or thoughts of any other parties. The authors and illustrator have represented and warrant full ownership and/or legal right to publish all the materials in this book.

Why Can't Every Day Be Daddy Day?
All Rights Reserved
Copyright ©2021 J. LaForte & J. Young
Cover Photo & All Photos by Arif Khan, Artist of India – All rights
reserved to J. LaForte & J. Young

This book may not be reproduced, transmitted, or stored in whole or in part by any means, including graphic, electronic, or mechanical without the express written consent of the publisher except in the case of brief quotations embodied in critical articles and reviews.

TwoJays Press d/b/a JoAnn LaForte
https://joannlaforte.com/
Paperback ISBN: 978-0-692-05406-2

TwoJays Press is a trademark belonging to J. LaForte & J. Young and JoAnn LaForte & https://joannlaforte.com/ are trademarks belonging to J. LaForte.
Printed in the United States of America

This book is dedicated
to the children of
the world
and we hope it makes
you smile.

Jonathan and Andy were the best of friends. They were 7 years old. They went to school together, played together, why, they did everything together!

One of the many things they had in common was they both lived only with their moms. Their dads did not live at home anymore. Sometimes this caused them to feel sad and confused.

They would talk about it, but they really did not know how to help each other. They were just young children, after all.

They began to think out loud together on one rainy afternoon.

It seemed they both shared the same experiences. Mommy crying, Daddy being silent, and sometimes, there was arguing. Jonathan and Andy agreed that all they wished for was that everyone would get along and be happy. They did not understand why anyone would have to be mean to each other.

Both of their dads were very loving and concerned. They only lived a few miles away from their moms, but to the boys, this distance seemed far away. They got to visit their dads sometimes, but it always became sad when it was time to be driven back home to Mom.

They would jump into their dads' cars every other weekend and enjoy the ride; so happy they were together again with their dads, who were also loving, protective, and so much fun!

Jonathan's dad drove a fun car and Andy's dad drove a pretty car. Jonathan and Andy would laugh at how their dads would compare their cars for what seemed like hours. The boys loved how their dads were friends too, just like they were.

When their parents were sad sometimes, Jonathan and Andy would laugh a lot and tried their best not to be sad, especially when they saw the frowns on their moms' and dads' faces.

They would tell each other stories and sing fun songs to help each other feel better.

Sometimes Andy was afraid to fall asleep at night in the dark, and sometimes Jonathan couldn't sleep at all. This made their parents sad.

On Mondays, they did their best to get up in the morning and go to school. They were not in the same class, but Jonathan and Andy would see each other in the lunch room and share lots of smiles and happy stories. Sometimes they got in trouble in their classrooms.

After school, sometimes Andy would be too tired to play soccer, and Jonathan would fall asleep at his baseball games. Their moms and dads became upset when they saw those little smiling faces which they loved so much, turn into frowns.

Jonathan and Andy would draw pictures in their art class about the fun things they did over the holidays, on weekends, at amusement parks and other special places when their dads would make their dreams come true.

These were special times and their moms would smile as their dads would drive up and then wave goodbye.

The best times, Jonathan and Andy decided, were when their grandmas came over. They would tell secret stories they didn't tell in school, to their grandmas, and they all would cry.

These were stories about how their moms and dads would fight sometimes and not be happy, and it made them all sad. Grandmas were sad the moms and dads were not living together and could not always get along. They understood and did their best to make Jonathan and Andy happy in other ways so they would forget their worries.

Grandmas were the best! Jonathan and Andy knew they could do anything with their grandmas because almost everything was allowed! They would laugh and smile and talk about those stories which made Jonathan and Andy sad, but grandmas would make all the tears disappear like magic!

Grandmas always made sure everything was comfortable for the boys. They could eat anything they want and could stay up late when grandmas had them over for visits. They wished their moms and dads could be like grandmas and simply happy all the time.

The grandmas had been talking to their moms and dads! They wanted the boys to stop worrying about their parents and asked them please do their best to get along and be friends.

Suddenly, one afternoon, Andy's mom had lunch together with his dad and her other family. There was a baby brother, baby sister and a kind stepdad in that family. All of them cheered together after that at the next soccer game. The coach was being tough with the team players because he wanted them to win, so Andy played his best.

Meanwhile, Jonathan's mom and dad were doing a lot of talking by themselves. They told him they had a big surprise. Jonathan would not have to see them at different times anymore because they would all live in the same home once again. This made Jonathan so happy! He began to smile all the time and called his grandma to tell her how happy he was.

Even though everyone seemed happier, Andy and Jonathan knew that not all of the kids in school could be so lucky.

What they did together after that was to pray hard to Jesus. "Please, Jesus, can all children smile, be happy, and feel that they are loved? It is not fair that the moms and dads are not always together. That does not matter, because moms and dads love their kids so much no matter where they live."

Andy and Jonathan wanted every little boy and girl to know how strong and happy they could be, and how the world they lived in was so beautiful. If moms and dads did not live in the same house, the love for their children is always close to them, right there, inside their little hearts.

The End.

Acknowledgements

JoAnn LaForte, besides being a published author of fictional romance stories, is a mom, grandma, good friend, daughter, sister, colleague, inspirational social media writer, artist, and photographer. Her dedication to share the secrets of success and happiness to the world is unstoppable. "By applying an attitude of positivity, gratitude and prayer to your everyday life, nothing is impossible." JoAnn's greatest passions are found within the beauty of nature, her sensitivity to the animal kingdom and her absolute adoration of the unconditional love found within children, the motivation for the writing of this story.

Joshua Young contributes a great deal to humanity without the need for recognition or praise. While exemplifying a strong personal commitment to family and friends, he is also a dedicated volunteer fire fighter, the esteemed member of the race control team at NASCAR, and a committed staff member at The New Testament Church and Mission. Josh is the creator of and assistant to his co-author, JoAnn, in their worldwide inspirational media page, has acted in the capacity of her marketing manager, writing assistant and most importantly, a loyal and patient friend. Perhaps his most honorable trait is the unconditional love and dedication he has for his son.

Arif Khan is an unbelievably talented and aspiring young artist who, in the opinion of both authors, will achieve his dreams of becoming incredibly important and successful in his native land of India and beyond. Through the inspirational page, Arif was recognized for a complimentary remark prompting the authors to investigate his profile. His profound headline stated, "I am as an artist; disconnect your mobile and reconnect with nature" marked the beginning of a cherished friendship and work relationship with the team. Arif is an exemplary person who loves God, life, family, friends, country, nature, and his craft. He is an insightful person who sees the beauty of the earth and all the wonderful things God has bestowed upon it, living his life to the fullest. His dedication and excitement while contributing his unique and colorful paintings to this story were beyond our expectations, and we are grateful and blessed.

Acknowledgements

Darby Oehl is a lovely young woman with a silence about herself that speaks louder than she thinks. Darby and JoAnn met by chance in a bookstore on the upper east side of Manhattan in 2017, obviously destined to be coworkers and friends. Darby's talents are more than what she believes about herself and the decision to retain her as the permanent editor was without reservation. Darby is seriously dedicated and meticulous in all her endeavors; thorough, honest, comforting, understanding, patient, and above all, shows a strong loyalty to everyone in her life. Her editing services in this children's story are a crucial part to the success we prayerfully anticipate.

Kim Munro. The amazing thing about positivity and gratitude is, 'the more you give it, the more you get back.' The final stage of publication brought us a much-needed miracle. Amidst a few bumps in the road and frustrating halts in production, along came Kim, a talented and amazing self-starter, who adopted our project with much enthusiasm and dedication. Kim is a loyal, accommodating, and positive person who goes above and beyond to provide complete satisfaction to her customers. She is a wife, daughter, mother, sister, and friend, but most especially, we are proud she is now part of our team, and our gratitude is overwhelming for a job extraordinarily done!

www.ingramcontent.com/pod-product-compliance
Lightning Source LLC
Chambersburg PA
CBHW050852010526

44107CB00047BA/1581